# THELONIOUS MONK

## Play-Along

Don Sickler - Trumpet
Ronnie Matthews - Piano
Kiyoshi Kitagawa - Bass
Ben Riley – Drums

Recorded, mixed, and mastered by Rudy Van Gelder,
Van Gelder Recording Studio, Inc.

To access online content visit:
**www.halleonard.com/mylibrary**

**Enter Code**
**1385-5066-9164-2884**

ISBN 978-1-4950-9300-5

## HAL•LEONARD®

For more information on the Real Book series, including community forums, please visit
**www.OfficialRealBook.com**

Visit Hal Leonard Online at
**www.halleonard.com**

Contact Us:
**Hal Leonard**
7777 West Bluemound Road
Milwaukee, WI 53213
Email: info@halleonard.com

In Europe contact:
**Hal Leonard Europe Limited**
Distribution Centre, Newmarket Road
Bury St Edmunds, Suffolk, IP33 3YB
Email: info@halleonardeurope.com

In Australia contact:
**Hal Leonard Australia Pty. Ltd.**
4 Lentara Court
Cheltenham, Victoria, 3192 Australia
Email: info@halleonard.com.au

# Contents

# BEMSHA SWING

-THELONIOUS MONK/DENZIL BEST

# Blue Monk

C VERSION

— THELONIOUS MONK

LAST X,
REPEAT HEAD IN/OUT

# GREEN CHIMNEYS

C Version

– THELONIOUS MONK

# REFLECTIONS

(Ballad)

—Thelonious Monk

C Version

* MONK'S "BENT" NOTE

** SOLO CHANGES

LAST X,

*** AFTER SOLO, PLAY A°7, THEN D.S.

# RHYTHM-A-NING

-Thelonious Monk

C Version

# STRAIGHT NO CHASER

(Fast Blues)

— THELONIOUS MONK

C VERSION

AFTER SOLOS, D.S. AL ⊕
(PLAY PICKUP) (TAKE REPEAT)

# UGLY BEAUTY

— THELONIOUS MONK

(MED. SLOW SWING)

C VERSION

RIT. LAST X

LAST X, FINE

\* BOTH THE ♮5 AND ♭5 ARE VOICED IN THE HARMONY: THE ♮5 ABOVE THE ROOT, BELOW THE ♭5.

# BEMSHA SWING

-Thelonious Monk/Denzil Best

Bb Version

# Blue Monk

(MED. SWING)

Bb VERSION

— THELONIOUS MONK

LAST X,
REPEAT HEAD IN/OUT

# Green Chimneys

B♭ Version

– Thelonious Monk

# Reflections

**D** SOLO (1st & 2nd x)
"RHYTHM CHANGES"
C ( D⁻⁷  D#°⁷  E⁻⁷  A⁷  D⁻⁷  G⁷ )

C⁷  F⁷  C⁷

**E** E⁷  A⁷

D⁷  G⁷

**F** C⁷ ( D⁻⁷  D#°⁷  E⁻⁷  A⁷  D⁻⁷  G⁷ )

C⁷  F⁷  C⁷

1st X, BACK TO **D** WITH REPEAT
2nd X, TO **G**

**G** SOLO (3rd & 4th x)
G#⁷  C#⁷  F#⁷  B⁷  E⁷  A⁷  D⁷  G⁷

C⁷

**H** E⁷  A⁷

D⁷  G⁷

**I** G#⁷  C#⁷  F#⁷  B⁷  E⁷  A⁷  D⁷  G⁷

C⁷  F⁷  C⁷

1st X, BACK TO **G** WITH REPEAT
2nd X, D.C. AL FINE

# 'Round Midnight

-Thelonious Monk/Cootie Williams/Bernie Hanighen

(Ballad)

Bb Version

# Straight No Chaser

— Thelonious Monk

AFTER SOLOS, D.S. AL ⊕
(PLAY PICKUP) (TAKE REPEAT)

# Ugly Beauty

— Thelonious Monk

RIT. LAST X

LAST X,
FINE

\* BOTH THE ♮5 AND ♭5 ARE VOICED IN THE HARMONY: THE ♮5 ABOVE THE ROOT, BELOW THE ♭5.

AFTER SOLO, D.S. AL FINE

# BEMSHA SWING

-Thelonious Monk / Denzil Best

# Blue Monk

— Thelonious Monk

# GREEN CHIMNEYS

Eb Version

— Thelonious Monk

# MONK'S DREAM

BY THELONIOUS MONK

# REFLECTIONS

—Thelonious Monk

(BALLAD)

Eb Version

* MONK'S "BENT" NOTE

** SOLO CHANGES

LAST X, 𝄐
*** AFTER SOLO, PLAY F#°7, THEN D.S.

(UP SWING)

# RHYTHM-A-NING

-Thelonious Monk

Eb Version

SOLO (1st & 2nd x)
"RHYTHM CHANGES"

1st X, BACK TO D WITH REPEAT
2nd X, TO G

SOLO (3rd & 4th x)

1st X, BACK TO G WITH REPEAT
2nd X, D.C. AL FINE

# 'Round Midnight

-Thelonious Monk/Cootie Williams/Bernie Hanighen

# Straight No Chaser

- Thelonious Monk

# Ugly Beauty

— Thelonious Monk

* BOTH THE ♮5 AND ♭5 ARE VOICED IN THE HARMONY: THE ♮5 ABOVE THE ROOT, BELOW THE ♭5.

AFTER SOLO, D.S. AL FINE

# BEMSHA SWING

-Thelonious Monk/Denzil Best

# Blue Monk

— Thelonious Monk

LAST X,
REPEAT HEAD IN/OUT

# Bright Mississippi

—Thelonious Monk

# Green Chimneys

— THELONIOUS MONK

C BASS VERSION

AFTER SOLOS, D.S. AL ⊕

# REFLECTIONS

-Thelonious Monk

C BASS VERSION

* MONK'S "BENT" NOTE

** SOLO CHANGES

LAST X, 𝄐
*** AFTER SOLO, PLAY A°7, THEN D.S.

# RHYTHM-A-NING

-Thelonious Monk

C BASS VERSION

# 'Round Midnight

-Thelonious Monk/Cootie Williams/Bernie Hanighen

C BASS VERSION

LAST X,
FINE
AFTER SOLOS, D.S. AL FINE

# Straight No Chaser

(FAST BLUES)

C BASS VERSION

— THELONIOUS MONK

AFTER SOLOS, D.S. AL ⊕
(PLAY PICKUP) (TAKE REPEAT)

# UGLY BEAUTY

— THELONIOUS MONK

C BASS VERSION

RIT. LAST X

LAST X,
FINE

\* BOTH THE ♯5 AND ♭5 ARE VOICED IN THE HARMONY: THE ♯5 ABOVE THE ROOT, BELOW THE ♭5.

AFTER SOLO, D.S. AL FINE

# THE REAL BOOK MULTI-TRACKS

## 1. MAIDEN VOYAGE PLAY-ALONG
Autumn Leaves • Blue Bossa • Doxy • Footprints • Maiden Voyage • Now's the Time • On Green Dolphin Street • Satin Doll • Summertime • Tune Up.
00196616 Book with Online Media.................................................................$17.99

## 2. MILES DAVIS PLAY-ALONG
Blue in Green • Boplicity (Be Bop Lives) • Four • Freddie Freeloader • Milestones • Nardis • Seven Steps to Heaven • So What • Solar • Walkin'.
00196798 Book with Online Media.................................................................$17.99

## 3. ALL BLUES PLAY-ALONG
All Blues • Back at the Chicken Shack • Billie's Bounce (Bill's Bounce) • Birk's Works • Blues by Five • C-Jam Blues • Mr. P.C. • One for Daddy-O • Reunion Blues • Turnaround.
00196692 Book with Online Media.................................................................$17.99

## 4. CHARLIE PARKER PLAY-ALONG
Anthropology • Blues for Alice • Confirmation • Donna Lee • K.C. Blues • Moose the Mooche • My Little Suede Shoes • Ornithology • Scrapple from the Apple • Yardbird Suite.
00196799 Book with Online Media.................................................................$17.99

## 5. JAZZ FUNK PLAY-ALONG
Alligator Bogaloo • The Chicken • Cissy Strut • Cold Duck Time • Comin' Home Baby • Mercy, Mercy, Mercy • Put It Where You Want It • Sidewinder • Tom Cat • Watermelon Man.
00196728 Book with Online Media.................................................................$17.99

## 6. SONNY ROLLINS PLAY-ALONG
Airegin • Blue Seven • Doxy • Duke of Iron • Oleo • Pent up House • St. Thomas • Sonnymoon for Two • Strode Rode • Tenor Madness.
00218264 Book with Online Media.................................................................$17.99

## 9. CHRISTMAS CLASSICS
Blue Christmas • Christmas Time Is Here • Frosty the Snow Man • Have Yourself a Merry Little Christmas • I'll Be Home for Christmas • My Favorite Things • Santa Claus Is Comin' to Town • Silver Bells • White Christmas • Winter Wonderland.
00236808 Book with Online Media.................................................................$17.99

## 8. BEBOP ERA PLAY-ALONG
Au Privave • Boneology • Bouncing with Bud • Dexterity • Groovin' High • Half Nelson • In Walked Bud • Lady Bird • Move • Witches Pit.
00196728 Book with Online Media.................................................................$17.99

## 10. CHRISTMAS SONGS
Away in a Manger • The First Noel • Go, Tell It on the Mountain • Hark! the Herald Angels Sing • Jingle Bells • Joy to the World • O Come, All Ye Faithful • O Holy Night • Up on the Housetop • We Wish You a Merry Christmas.
00236809 Book with Online Media.................................................................$17.99

The interactive, online audio interface includes:
- tempo control
- looping
- buttons to turn each instrument on or off
- lead sheet with follow-along marker
- melody performed by a saxophone or trumpet on the "head in" and "head out."

The full stereo tracks can also be downloaded and played off-line. Separate lead sheets are included for C, B-flat, E-flat and Bass Clef instruments.

HAL•LEONARD®
www.halleonard.com

Prices, content and availability subject to change without notice.

# The Best-Selling Jazz Book of All Time Is Now Legal!

The Real Books are the most popular jazz books of all time. Since the 1970s, musicians have trusted these volumes to get them through every gig, night after night. The problem is that the books were illegally produced and distributed, without any regard to copyright law, or royalties paid to the composers who created these musical masterpieces.

Hal Leonard is very proud to present the first legitimate and legal editions of these books ever produced. You won't even notice the difference, other than all the notorious errors being fixed: the covers and typeface look the same, the song lists are nearly identical, and the price for our edition is even cheaper than the originals!

Every conscientious musician will appreciate that these books are now produced accurately and ethically, benefitting the songwriters that we owe for some of the greatest tunes of all time!

## VOLUME 1
| | | |
|---|---|---|
| 00240221 | C Edition | $39.99 |
| 00240224 | B♭ Edition | $39.99 |
| 00240225 | E♭ Edition | $39.99 |
| 00240226 | Bass Clef Edition | $39.99 |
| 00240292 | C Edition 6 x 9 | $35.00 |
| 00240339 | B♭ Edition 6 x 9 | $35.00 |
| 00147792 | Bass Clef Edition 6 x 9 | $35.00 |
| 00451087 | C Edition on CD-ROM | $29.99 |
| 00200984 | Online Backing Tracks: Selections | $45.00 |
| 00110604 | Book/USB Flash Drive Backing Tracks Pack | $79.99 |
| 00110599 | USB Flash Drive Only | $50.00 |

## VOLUME 2
| | | |
|---|---|---|
| 00240222 | C Edition | $39.99 |
| 00240227 | B♭ Edition | $39.99 |
| 00240228 | E♭ Edition | $39.99 |
| 00240229 | Bass Clef Edition | $39.99 |
| 00240293 | C Edition 6 x 9 | $35.00 |
| 00125900 | B♭ Edition 6 x 9 | $35.00 |
| 00451088 | C Edition on CD-ROM | $30.99 |
| 00125900 | The Real Book – Mini Edition | $35.00 |
| 00204126 | Backing Tracks on USB Flash Drive | $50.00 |
| 00204131 | C Edition – USB Flash Drive Pack | $79.99 |

## VOLUME 3
| | | |
|---|---|---|
| 00240233 | C Edition | $39.99 |
| 00240284 | B♭ Edition | $39.99 |
| 00240285 | E♭ Edition | $39.99 |
| 00240286 | Bass Clef Edition | $39.99 |
| 00240338 | C Edition 6 x 9 | $35.00 |
| 00451089 | C Edition on CD-ROM | $29.99 |

## VOLUME 4
| | | |
|---|---|---|
| 00240296 | C Edition | $39.99 |
| 00103348 | B♭ Edition | $39.99 |
| 00103349 | E♭ Edition | $39.99 |
| 00103350 | Bass Clef Edition | $39.99 |

## VOLUME 5
| | | |
|---|---|---|
| 00240349 | C Edition | $39.99 |
| 00175278 | B♭ Edition | $39.99 |
| 00175279 | E♭ Edition | $39.99 |

## VOLUME 6
| | | |
|---|---|---|
| 00240534 | C Edition | $39.99 |
| 00223637 | E♭ Edition | $39.99 |

*Also available:*
| | | |
|---|---|---|
| 00154230 | The Real Bebop Book | $34.99 |
| 00240264 | The Real Blues Book | $34.99 |
| 00310910 | The Real Bluegrass Book | $32.50 |
| 00240223 | The Real Broadway Book | $35.00 |
| 00240440 | The Trane Book | $22.99 |
| 00125426 | The Real Country Book | $39.99 |
| 00240355 | The Real Dixieland Book C Edition | $32.50 |
| 00122335 | The Real Dixieland Book B♭ Edition | $32.50 |
| 00240235 | The Duke Ellington Real Book | $19.99 |
| 00240268 | The Real Jazz Solos Book | $30.00 |
| 00240348 | The Real Latin Book C Edition | $37.50 |
| 00127107 | The Real Latin Book B♭ Edition | $35.00 |
| 00120809 | The Pat Metheny Real Book | $24.99 |
| 00240358 | The Charlie Parker Real Book | $19.99 |
| 00118324 | The Real Pop Book – Vol. 1 | $35.00 |
| 00240331 | The Bud Powell Real Book | $19.99 |
| 00240437 | The Real R&B Book | $39.99 |
| 00240313 | The Real Rock Book | $35.00 |
| 00240323 | The Real Rock Book – Vol. 2 | $35.00 |
| 00240359 | The Real Tab Book | $32.50 |
| 00240317 | The Real Worship Book | $29.99 |

## THE REAL CHRISTMAS BOOK
| | | |
|---|---|---|
| 00240306 | C Edition | $32.50 |
| 00240345 | B♭ Edition | $32.50 |
| 00240346 | E♭ Edition | $32.50 |
| 00240347 | Bass Clef Edition | $32.50 |
| 00240431 | A-G CD Backing Tracks | $24.99 |
| 00240432 | H-M CD Backing Tracks | $24.99 |
| 00240433 | N-Y CD Backing Tracks | $24.99 |

## THE REAL VOCAL BOOK
| | | |
|---|---|---|
| 00240230 | Volume 1 High Voice | $35.00 |
| 00240307 | Volume 1 Low Voice | $35.00 |
| 00240231 | Volume 2 High Voice | $35.00 |
| 00240308 | Volume 2 Low Voice | $35.00 |
| 00240391 | Volume 3 High Voice | $35.00 |
| 00240392 | Volume 3 Low Voice | $35.00 |
| 00118318 | Volume 4 High Voice | $35.00 |
| 00118319 | Volume 4 Low Voice | $35.00 |

## THE REAL BOOK – STAFF PAPER
| | |
|---|---|
| 00240327 | $10.99 |

## HOW TO PLAY FROM A REAL BOOK
| | |
|---|---|
| 00312097 | $17.50 |

## THE REAL BOOK – ENHANCED CHORDS
| | |
|---|---|
| 00151290 | $29.99 |

**Complete song lists online at www.halleonard.com**

# ♯HAL•LEONARD®
7777 W. BLUEMOUND RD. P.O. BOX 13819 MILWAUKEE, WI 53213

*Prices, content, and availability subject to change without notice.*

0318

# Presenting the Hal Leonard JAZZ PLAY-ALONG SERIES

For use with all B-flat, E-flat, Bass Clef and C instruments, the Jazz Play-Along® Series is the ultimate learning tool for all jazz musicians. With musician-friendly lead sheets, melody cues, and other split-track audio choices included, these first-of-a-kind packages help you master improvisation while playing some of the greatest tunes of all time. FOR STUDY, each tune includes a split track with: melody cue with proper style and inflection • professional rhythm tracks • choruses for soloing • removable bass part • removable piano part. FOR PERFORMANCE, each tune also has: an additional full stereo accompaniment track (no melody) • additional choruses for soloing.

*These do not include split tracks.

0418

# Jazz Instruction & Improvisation

## BOOKS FOR ALL INSTRUMENTS FROM HAL LEONARD

### AN APPROACH TO JAZZ IMPROVISATION
*by Dave Pozzi*
*Musicians Institute Press*
Explore the styles of Charlie Parker, Sonny Rollins, Bud Powell and others with this comprehensive guide to jazz improvisation. Covers: scale choices • chord analysis • phrasing • melodies • harmonic progressions • more.
00695135 Book/CD Pack......................$17.95

### THE ART OF MODULATING
FOR PIANISTS AND JAZZ MUSICIANS
*by Carlos Salzedo &*
*Lucile Lawrence*
*Schirmer*
*The Art of Modulating* is a treatise originally intended for the harp, but this edition has been edited for use by intermediate keyboardists and other musicians who have an understanding of basic music theory. In its pages you will find: table of intervals; modulation rules; modulation formulas; examples of modulation; extensions and cadences; ten fragments of dances; five characteristic pieces; and more.
50490581 ..............................$19.99

### BUILDING A JAZZ VOCABULARY
*By Mike Steinel*
A valuable resource for learning the basics of jazz from Mike Steinel of the University of North Texas. It covers: the basics of jazz • how to build effective solos • a comprehensive practice routine • and a jazz vocabulary of the masters.
00849911 ..............................$19.99

### THE CYCLE OF FIFTHS
*by Emile and Laura De Cosmo*
This essential instruction book provides more than 450 exercises, including hundreds of melodic and rhythmic ideas. The book is designed to help improvisors master the cycle of fifths, one of the primary progressions in music. Guaranteed to refine technique, enhance improvisational fluency, and improve sight-reading!
00311114 ..............................$16.99

### THE DIATONIC CYCLE
*by Emile and Laura De Cosmo*
Renowned jazz educators Emile and Laura De Cosmo provide more than 300 exercises to help improvisors tackle one of music's most common progressions: the diatonic cycle. This book is guaranteed to refine technique, enhance improvisational fluency, and improve sight-reading!
00311115 ..............................$16.95

### EAR TRAINING
*by Keith Wyatt,*
*Carl Schroeder and Joe Elliott*
*Musicians Institute Press*
Covers: basic pitch matching • singing major and minor scales • identifying intervals • transcribing melodies and rhythm • identifying chords and progressions • seventh chords and the blues • modal interchange, chromaticism, modulation • and more.
00695198 Book/Online Audio ..............................$24.99

### EXERCISES AND ETUDES FOR THE JAZZ INSTRUMENTALIST
*by J.J. Johnson*
Designed as study material and playable by any instrument, these pieces run the gamut of the jazz experience, featuring common and uncommon time signatures and keys, and styles from ballads to funk. They are progressively graded so that both beginners and professionals will be challenged by the demands of this wonderful music.
00842018 Bass Clef Edition ..............................$17.99
00842042 Treble Clef Edition ..............................$16.95

### JAZZOLOGY
THE ENCYCLOPEDIA OF JAZZ THEORY FOR ALL MUSICIANS
*by Robert Rawlins and*
*Nor Eddine Bahha*
This comprehensive resource covers a variety of jazz topics, for beginners and pros of any instrument. The book serves as an encyclopedia for reference, a thorough methodology for the student, and a workbook for the classroom.
00311167 ..............................$19.99

### JAZZ THEORY RESOURCES
*by Bert Ligon*
*Houston Publishing, Inc.*
This is a jazz theory text in two volumes. **Volume 1 includes**: review of basic theory • rhythm in jazz performance • triadic generalization • diatonic harmonic progressions and analysis • substitutions and turnarounds • and more. **Volume 2 includes**: modes and modal frameworks • quartal harmony • extended tertian structures and triadic superimposition • pentatonic applications • coloring "outside" the lines and beyond • and more.
00030458 Volume 1 ..............................$39.95
00030459 Volume 2 ..............................$29.95

### HAL•LEONARD®
7777 W. BLUEMOUND RD. P.O. BOX 13819 MILWAUKEE, WI 53213

Visit Hal Leonard online at
**www.halleonard.com**

### JOY OF IMPROV
*by Dave Frank*
*and John Amaral*
This book/audio course on improvisation for all instruments and all styles will help players develop monster musical skills! Book One imparts a solid basis in technique, rhythm, chord theory, ear training and improv concepts. **Book Two** explores more advanced chord voicings, chord arranging techniques and more challenging blues and melodic lines. The audio can be used as a listening and play-along tool.
00220005 Book 1 – Book/Online Audio ..............$27.99
00220006 Book 2 – Book/Online Audio ..............$26.99

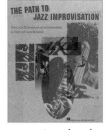

### THE PATH TO JAZZ IMPROVISATION
*by Emile and Laura De Cosmo*
This fascinating jazz instruction book offers an innovative, scholarly approach to the art of improvisation. It includes in-depth analysis and lessons about: cycle of fifths • diatonic cycle • overtone series • pentatonic scale • harmonic and melodic minor scale • polytonal order of keys • blues and bebop scales • modes • and more.
00310904 ..............................$14.99

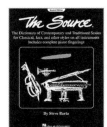

### THE SOURCE
THE DICTIONARY OF CONTEMPORARY AND TRADITIONAL SCALES
*by Steve Barta*
This book serves as an informative guide for people who are looking for good, solid information regarding scales, chords, and how they work together. It provides right and left hand fingerings for scales, chords, and complete inversions. Includes over 20 different scales, each written in all 12 keys.
00240885 ..............................$19.99

### 21 BEBOP EXERCISES
*by Steve Rawlins*
This book/CD pack is both a warm-up collection and a manual for bebop phrasing. Its tasty and sophisticated exercises will help you develop your proficiency with jazz interpretation. It concentrates on practice in all twelve keys – moving higher by half-step – to help develop dexterity and range. The companion CD includes all of the exercises in 12 keys.
00315341 Book/CD Pack......................$17.95

Prices, contents & availability
subject to change without notice.

0417